Reader's Digest Kids™

Published by The Reader's Digest Association, Inc.

Created and produced by David Bennett Books Limited

Text copyright © 1992 Sally Grindley
Illustrations copyright © 1992 Stuart Trotter

Library of Congress Cataloging in Publication Data

Reader's Digest children's book of animals / written by Sally Grindley;
  illustrated by Stuart Trotter.
          p.   cm.
     Summary: Introduces the behavior and habitats of a variety of
  domestic and wild animals.
     ISBN 0-89577-443-7
     1. Animals—Miscellanea—Juvenile literature.   2. Domestic
  animals—Miscellanea—Juvenile literature.   [1. Animals—
  Miscellanea.]   I. Grindley, Sally.   II. Trotter, Stuart, ill.
  III. Reader's Digest Association.   IV. Title: Children's book of
  animals.
  QL49.R39   1992
  591—dc20   92-15234
                                                          CIP
                                                           AC

READER'S DIGEST and the Pegasus logo are registered trademarks of
          The Reader's Digest Association, Inc.

Printed in Singapore

Reader's Digest Fund for the Blind is publisher of the Large-Type Edition of *Reader's
Digest*. For subscription information about this magazine, please contact Reader's
Digest Fund for the Blind, Inc., Dept. 250, Pleasantville, N.Y. 10570.

Reader's Digest™

Reader's Digest
Children's Book of
Animals

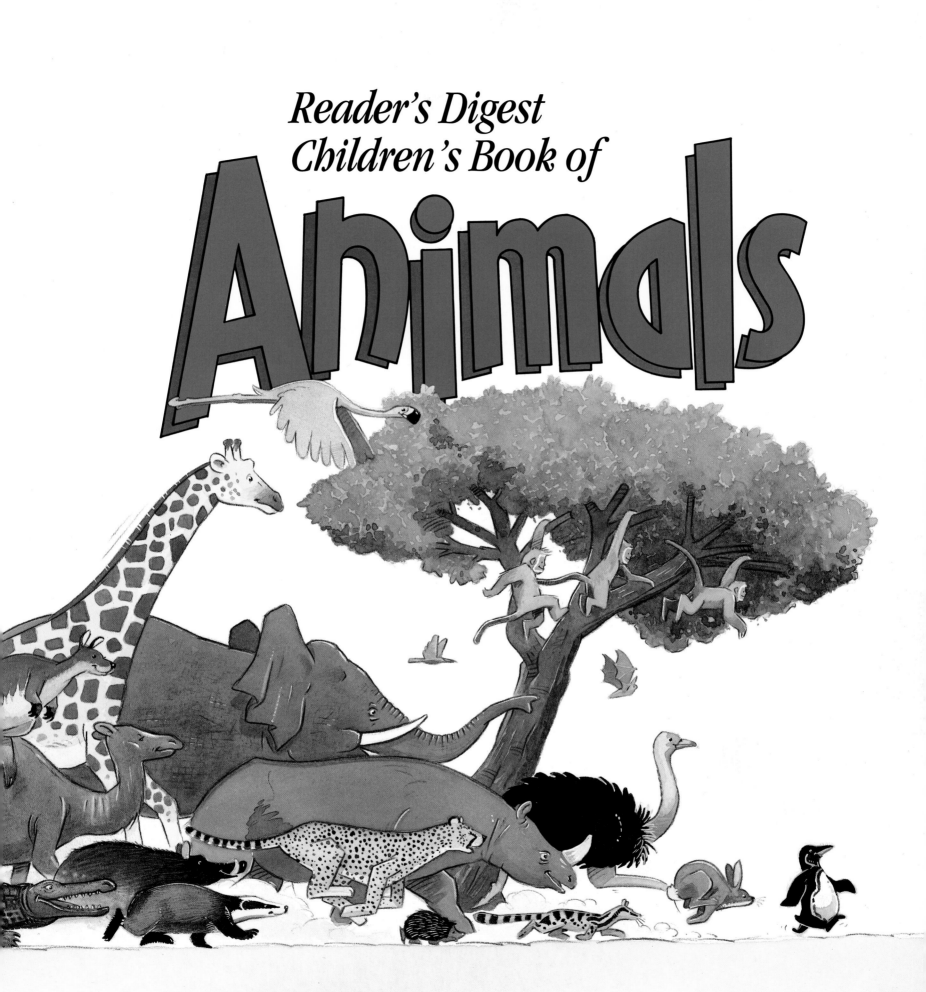

Written by Sally Grindley • Illustrated by Stuart Trotter

READER'S DIGEST KIDS

Pleasantville, N.Y.—Montreal

Contents

All Sorts Of Animals

rabbit

Mammals

Mammals always have hair or fur, and they all breathe air. Because they are warm-blooded, their bodies stay the same temperature when the weather is hot or cold. Mammal mothers feed their newborn babies milk.

dolphin

polar bear

gorilla

kingfisher

Birds

Birds, like mammals, are warm-blooded. But instead of fur or hair, they have feathers and wings. A bird's beak helps it catch food. But because it has no teeth, it swallows its food whole. Mother birds lay eggs.

penguin

frigate bird

macaw

cichlid fish

Fish

eel

Fish lay eggs as birds do. But since fish are cold-blooded, their body temperature changes to match the temperature of the water. Fish swim by moving their fins.

common carp

manta ray

Insects

Insects always have six legs, two feelers and a three-part body. Often they also have one or two pairs of wings.

dragonfly

bumblebee

butterfly

ladybug

Amphibians

Amphibians live both in water and on land. These cold-blooded animals lay their eggs in water, but often live on land as adults. Most amphibians breathe through their skin.

frog

Reptiles

Reptiles, like amphibians, are cold-blooded creatures that lay eggs. Reptiles wear scaly, watertight skins. They usually feed on other smaller animals.

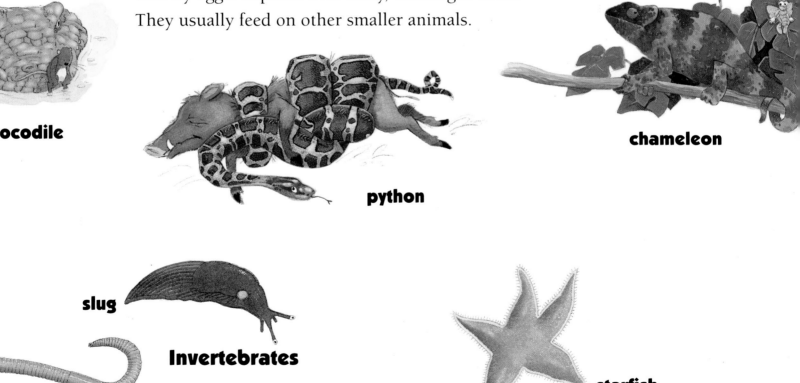

crocodile

python

chameleon

slug

Invertebrates

Invertebrates have no bones; so often they are soft and squishy. Some live in a hard shell that protects them. They are found on land or in the water. All invertebrates lay eggs.

worm

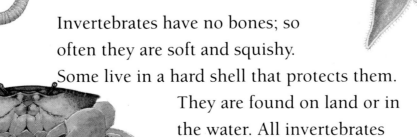
crab

starfish

snail

In The Garden

Look for the **caterpillar** munching leaves. Once it is big and fat, it will build a cocoon around itself. There it will stay until it changes into a butterfly.

This **butterfly** flutters around the garden in early spring. It feeds on the nectar inside flowers.

Ants almost never stop moving. They hurry from place to place, collecting food, and building their nest.

A **woodlouse** lives in cool, damp places, where it eats rotting wood and leaves. When touched, it may roll into a tight ball for protection.

Gardeners like the beetle called a **ladybug**. It eats greenflies, which damage plants and vegetables.

A **wasp** eats fruit and other sweet food. It uses its sting only when bothered.

The **spider** spins a web of sticky silk to trap flying insects. It wraps them in its silk before it eats them.

Here's a creature that carries its house on its back! The **snail's** shell protects it from the sun and from animals that want to eat it.

Slugs leave a silvery trail of slime wherever they go. Gardeners don't like them, because they gobble up flowers and vegetables.

Bumblebees buzz from flower to flower on warm, sunny days. They gather the nectar inside flowers and carry it back to their nest.

During the day, the **ground beetle** hides under stones in the garden. In the evening, it comes out to hunt, especially for snails.

11

On The Farm

Cows live in the fields for most of the year, eating grass and hay. They move into the barn for the winter. People drink the cows' milk and make cheese and butter from it.

Hens lay the eggs that many people eat. At night, the hens stay in a wooden house called a coop where they are kept warm and safe.

Some people keep **horses** to ride or to pull carts. When the horses are not in the fields or a fenced yard, they live in a stable.

The **rooster** wakes the whole farmyard every early morning..

All day long, **sheep** munch and munch the farmyard grass. The farmer shears off their woolly coats in summer. Then people use the wool to make winter clothes.

13

In Ponds And Marshes

The **duck** glides smoothly along the surface of the pond. But when it is hungry, it dives its head underwater, sticks its tail feathers up, and sifts the pond water for small fish and insects.

The **water boatman** swims on its back just under the pond's surface. Its legs act like a pair of oars to help move it along.

The **great diving beetle** can swim and fly. In the water, it traps a bubble of air under its wing cases to keep it from sinking.

Water voles live along the water's edge in nests called burrows. Voles not only swim well, they dive!

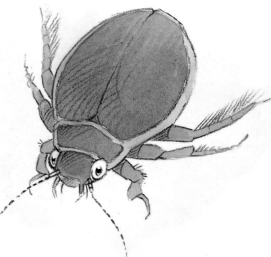

The **crested newt** sleeps the winter away on land. In spring, it returns to a pond to lay its eggs.

The **reed warbler** builds its nest among the reeds at the edge of ponds and marshes. There it catches and eats its favorite insects.

The **dragonfly** hovers over ponds and rivers, hunting for other flying insects. Its huge eyes help it to see all around.

Every spring, **frogs** lay hundreds of eggs in a jelly called spawn, which floats in the pond water. The eggs hatch into **tadpoles**, and the tadpoles gradually grow into frogs.

Common **toads** live most of the year away from water. But in the spring, they visit the ponds to breed and lay their eggs.

The **carp** can live for forty years and grow to be quite large. Most of the time, it sifts through the mud at the bottom of the pond looking food.

15

Underground

Ants live in underground nests made of many small rooms joined by passageways. They make special rooms where they lay their eggs.

Earthworms make tunnels through the soil by eating it as they go. They also eat dead leaves.

A **mole** almost never comes above ground. Its sharp-clawed feet are perfect for all the digging it does. You can tell where it has been by the piles of earth it leaves behind.

The **rabbit** usually stays underground during the day and hops out at night to find food. It digs a burrow to live in. Many burrows together are called a warren.

The **badger** keeps its underground home, called a set, very clean. It even changes its bedding every day.

The **fennec** is a fox that lives in hot deserts in Africa. It spends the day in its burrow. At night when it is cooler, it comes out to hunt.

Prairie dogs dig whole towns of underground tunnels. Several hundred of them may live in one town.

The **Australian desert frog** sleeps in its underground burrow almost all the time. It comes out only when the rains come, which is about once a year!

In The Treetops

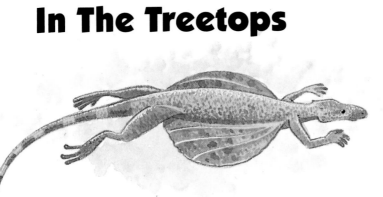

Flaps of skin between the **draco lizard's** front and back legs help it glide from tree to tree. It uses its tail to steer.

Watch out—that branch might be a snake! The **African vine snake** pretends to be a branch and waits for a bird to land on it. The bird quickly becomes the snake's dinner.

The **squirrel** scampers through the trees. Its long tail helps it balance.

The **gibbon** can swing through the trees faster than a person can run along the ground. It flings itself from branch to branch using its long arms and strong hands.

The **linsang** sometimes looks like a poisonous snake as it glides along branches, searching for food.

The **sugar glider** leaps from tree to tree. The flaps of skin between its front and back legs act like a parachute to keep it in the air.

The **koala** climbs high into the trees by digging its sharp claws into the bark. It is fussy about its food and will eat only the leaves of eucalyptus and gum trees.

The **orangutan** is the largest tree animal. Its name means 'old man of the forest.' It lives alone, or with a few other orangutans.

The **tree frog** uses special pads on its fingers and toes to climb trees. It can leap into the air to catch an insect, then glide to another tree.

Out At Night

The cries that the **bushbaby** makes at night sound just like a human baby's. It has extremely strong hearing that helps it find its food in the dark. It can even hear insects moving!

At night, the **dormouse** busily feeds on nuts, seeds and insects. By day, it sleeps in a little ball of grass, moss and leaves in a tree, or underneath a pile of leaves.

The **bat** makes clicking noises as it flies along. Then it listens for the echoes from these clicks to find obstacles in its way, and to catch food. During the day, it hangs upside down by its feet, fast asleep.

The **red fox** often prowls for food at night. With its good hearing, it finds small mammals, birds and insects. Its sense of smell sometimes leads it to food in people's garbage.

The **tarsier** uses its huge eyes to see in the dark. It leaps like a frog through the trees, searching for insects, eggs and lizards to eat. When it lands, its sticky toe pads help it grip the tree trunks securely.

The **raccoon** comes out at night to hunt for its food. It eats all sorts of animals, which it catches both on land and in the water. Sometimes it will even take the lid off a garbage can to look for leftovers.

The **wild boar**, a kind of pig, feeds mainly on acorns, beech nuts and roots dug up from the forest floor. Baby boars have striped fur that hides them in the forest at night.

The **hedgehog** makes a lot of noise. But that doesn't stop it from catching and eating insects and slugs. If it is threatened, the hedgehog rolls up into a tight ball so that its prickles protect it on all sides.

Along The Lakes And Rivers

The **salmon** lives in the sea. But when it is time to lay eggs, the salmon travels long distances up fresh water rivers. It will even leap high in the air to climb waterfalls.

The **kingfisher** perches on branches overhanging a river. If it sees a fish, it plunges into the water to catch it with its long, sharp beak.

Watch out for those claws! The **crayfish** uses them as tools to grab insect larvae, tadpoles and snails in the river bed at night.

In and out, in and out of the stream runs the **dipper**. It searches for small insects or fish to eat. It can even walk underwater along the bottom of the stream, or use its wings to swim.

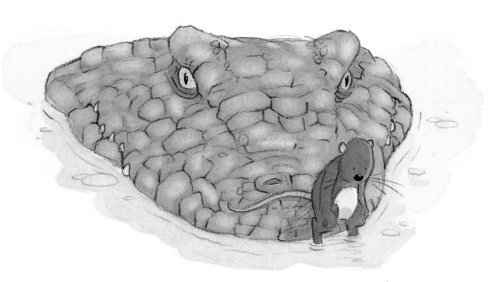

The **otter's** webbed back feet help it swim fast and catch fish easily. Because it comes out only at night, people rarely see it.

Danger! That **crocodile** looks like a log as it lies just below the surface of the water. It is waiting to pounce on some unsuspecting animal.

The **water opossum** hunts for fish along river bottoms. Even a water opossum mom with a pouch full of her babies can go into the river. The pouch closes up tight to keep water out.

The **hippo** often sits in a river with only its eyes and snout showing. It wallows in mud and water to keep cool and to stay out of reach of pesty insects.

23

Beside The Sea

Here's a fish that has no scales. Instead, the **blenny** has a slimy skin. It hides under stones and in tiny crevices in rock pools.

The **sea anemone** looks like a blob of jelly stuck to a rock. But when the sea covers it, the anemone pushes out tiny tentacles that wave around and trap small sea creatures. The tentacles also sting and paralyze the creatures, so the anemone can gobble them up whole.

A **prawn** is almost transparent. Only by looking carefully can people spot it swimming around in rock pools.

The **limpet** lives on seaside rocks and slowly moves backward and forward, eating the seaweed that grows there. It clings to its rock with such incredible strength, a person can't pull it loose.

The **acorn barnacle** holds tightly to its rock home. When the sea washes over it, it opens, and out comes a feathery foot to pull tiny bits of food from the water.

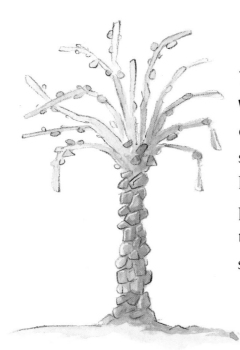

The **sand mason worm** uses grains of sand and bits of shell to build its home. Then it pokes out its tentacles to catch small sea creatures.

The **starfish** has no head, no feet and no hands! Yet its strong arms and suckers can force a shellfish open—impossible for a human hand!

The **hermit crab** moves into any empty spiral shell it can find and lives there. As it grows bigger, it moves into bigger and bigger shells. It often carries a sea anemone on its back, because the anemone's stinging tentacles can protect it from attackers.

The **crab** looks strange as it scuttles along sideways. When it outgrows its hard shell, it climbs out, and the soft, stretchy skin underneath hardens into a new shell.

Weird And Wonderful

Beware of the **Portuguese man-of-war**. The tentacles of this enormous jellyfish hang down in the water to sting and paralyze little fish. They can also sting people who come too close.

The **sea horse** swims upright, with a head like a horse's, and a tail that can grip like a monkey's. What is the seahorse? A fish!

The mother **eel** lays its eggs in deep sea water and then dies. When the young eels hatch, they must travel long distances to reach fresh water before they become adults. Sometimes they travel for two or three years.

The **lobster** needs its massive claws to fight its enemies or to crush food. If it loses one of its claws in a fight, it grows a new one!

The **manta ray** flaps its huge fins to move through the sea. It leaps completely out of the water, then lands with a loud belly flop. Although it is very large, it eats only small sea creatures.

Any fish that comes too near the **electric eel** is in for a shock! The electric eel gives off electricity that stuns the fish. Then the eel eats it.

This is no ordinary fish! When the **porcupine fish** is threatened, it blows itself up with water, which makes its body spines stick out. Attackers back off in a hurry!

The **octopus** has a huge head, and eight arms, each with many suckers. To catch its food, it swims up behind its prey and surprises it with an eight-armed hug.

Big And Blubbery

The **blue whale**, biggest of all animals, eats tiny sea creatures called krill deep in the water. It must come to the surface of the sea once in a while to breathe through the blowhole on top of its head.

Watch out!
Killer whales often hunt in large numbers. Their sharp pointed teeth allow them to eat fish, squid, penguins and seals.

The **walrus** roots along the sea bed to find food with its whiskery snout. It uses its two long tusks to pull itself out of the sea onto dry land or ice.

In the winter, the **Weddell seal** lives in freezing cold water under the ice. It makes breathing holes in the ice and keeps them open by chewing the edges with its teeth.

Dolphins speak to each other by making a series of different clicking noises. They find food and objects by listening to the echoes of their clicks.

Seals or **sea lions?** They look much alike. But sea lions have flaps over their ears that seals do not have. On land, sea lions turn their back flippers forward to help them move along. Seals cannot do this.

Bizarre Birds

The **hummingbird** flies forward, backward, sideways and even upside down. When it hovers to feed from a flower, it beats its wings too fast to see. But listen carefully and hear the hum!

Swifts spend all their time in flight. They can fly even while they sleep. They land only to lay eggs and raise their young.

The **pelican** uses its big, stretchy beak like a fishing net. It scoops up fish, then tilts its head to let the water drain away.

Many birds sing bird songs. But the **macaw** can imitate other songs as well. It is especially good at copying human voices.

What's making that noise behind the **owl's** back? The owl can turn its head almost completely around to find out! The owl sees perfectly in the dark. It spots small night animals such as mice, then flies silently to catch them.

Why does the **woodpecker** make its noisy rat-a-tat-tat? It drills into tree bark with its strong beak to build a nest hole, find insects, or tell other woodpeckers where it is.

Penguins may look silly when they waddle around on land. But on the snow, they zoom along on their tummies like living toboggans. They are also excellent swimmers.

Ostriches, the world's biggest birds, run as fast as racehorses. But they cannot fly!

Imagine how people would look if they turned the color of their food! **Flamingos** wear a coat of bright pink feathers that get their color from the shellfish the birds eat.

31

What A Way To Eat!

A **frigate bird** doesn't bother to catch its own food. It steals fish from other birds by chasing them until they drop their catch.

Who ever heard of an animal that eats with its nose? The **elephant's** long trunk has finger-like bumps on the end. When an elephant finds food, it picks it up with its trunk and pops it into its mouth.

A **camel** can go for weeks without drinking or eating. It stores fat in its hump and then uses it as food when it gets hungry.

The **anteater** pokes its long, sticky tongue into a termites' nest. Then it pulls the tongue out and eats the termites that are stuck to it.

A **chimpanzee** sometimes pokes a stick into a termites' nest, waits for the termites to climb onto it, and then licks them off.

The **giraffe**, with a neck almost as long as its legs, can reach the juicy leaves at the very top of a tree.

Often a **leopard** drags its dinner into a tree. There it can eat in peace, away from animals that might try to share its meal.

A **humpback** whale swims circles around fish, blowing a stream of bubbles through its blowhole to frighten them. When the fish huddle together, the whale gobbles them up in one gulp!

The **archer fish** watches for an insect clinging to an overhanging branch. Then it spits water at the insect, which tumbles into the water, where the fish snaps it up.

Master Builders

The queen **paper wasp** builds its nest with its mouth! The bee chews wood, then mixes it with saliva to make paste for building.

The tiny **termite** sometimes builds a nest that is taller than a person. It builds its nest of sand, clay and its own saliva. Inside the nest, it makes many rooms and passages.

A **satin bowerbird** not only builds its nest, it decorates it! Once it has shaped its nest in long grass, it searches for colorful bits and pieces to make the nest beautiful.

A **Siamese fighting fish** blows sticky bubbles to make its nest. The bubbles cling together on the water's surface. There among the bubbles, the fish can lay its eggs safely.

The clever **African weaver bird** twists long pieces of grass together to build its nest. But first, it attaches the nest firmly to the end of a twig.

No animal builds better than the **beaver**. If it cannot find water deep enough for its home, the beaver cuts down trees with its sharp teeth to build a dam across a stream. When the water forms a big pond behind the dam, the beaver builds its home, called a lodge, of mud and branches. It makes sure the front door is underwater.

A **potter wasp** scoops up balls of clay to shape into little pots. Then it fills the pots with caterpillars, and seals them up.

The **mountain gorilla** builds a new nest every night. It climbs a tree, bends branches and leaves around itself, and settles down to sleep. Sometimes, it builds a nest just to take a nap!

Honeybees make more than honey! They also make wax, which they use to build their honeycombs in hollow trees or beehives.

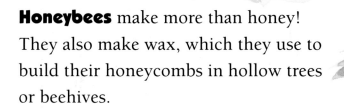

Now You See Me, Now You Don't

Look out! The **praying mantis** hides here, waiting to catch its next meal.

When danger approaches, the tiny **shrimpfish** hides among a sea urchin's sharp spines.

Watch your step! The **plaice** can change its colors to match the seabed where it hides.

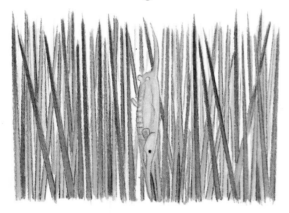

The common **snipe** wears stripes and spots to make it look like the grass where it sits.

In summer, a **ptarmigan's** feathers look spotty brown to match the forest. In winter, it turns white to blend with the snow.

Imagine playing hide-and-seek with a **chameleon**! It can change color to match almost anything near it!

As the **cuttlefish** swims above different colors on the seabed, it makes quick color changes to match each change in the background.

Which end is which? This **snake** coils itself up if attacked. Then it hides its head and raises its tail. The enemy attacks the wrong end!

When in danger, this **caterpillar** turns its body to show huge false eyes. This makes it look like a much bigger animal!

What color is a **stoat**? In summer, it hides in the undergrowth with a reddish brown coat. In winter, its coat turns white as the snow around it.

Sending Messages

Ring-tailed lemurs wave their tails to pass messages to each other. They hold their tails high in the air so that they can find one another more easily.

When a **honeybee** finds a new source of nectar, it returns to its hive. There it performs a special dance that shows other bees where to find the food.

This deadly **rattlesnake** shakes the rattle at the end of its tail to tell its enemies to stay away!

Danger! This **frog's** bright colors warn its enemies to leave it alone. It is covered with a very poisonous slime.

A male **elephant seal** opens his huge mouth wide to frighten other males away from his territory.

Birds leave this **hoverfly** alone because it looks like a wasp. But it is completely harmless. It doesn't even have a sting!

Pandas usually live alone, but they leave messages for other pandas by marking trees with scent from under their tails.

To fool an attacker, the **Virginia opossum** rolls over and lies completely still, sometimes for hours. The attacker thinks the opossum is dead and goes away.

A **peacock** attracts a peahen by opening wide all its tail feathers with their beautiful shiny "eyes".

39

Clean-Up Time

This **banded coral shrimp** plucks pests from the moray eel's skin. It also picks leftover food from the eel's teeth!

The **sloth** doesn't keep clean at all. It even has tiny green plants growing on its fur. The green color makes the sloth very difficult to see in the trees.

The **jaguar** licks itself all over to keep its fur clean and untangled.

The **oxpecker** perches on the backs of hippos, warthogs and giraffes. There it can feast on tasty ticks and flies. The large animals don't mind because the ticks and flies bother them.

Baboons keep each other clean. They spend much of their day stroking each other's fur, picking out seeds, dirt and lice.

Cleaner fish eat pests and dead skin from the bodies of much larger fish. Cleaner fish can even work inside the mouth of a shark, and it won't eat them!

The **pangolin** loves eating ants. But it also lets the ants crawl under its scales to eat the tiny bugs that live there.

An **elephant** sucks water into its trunk. Then it sprays itself all over to get rid of pests and dirt, and to cool off. Mom will squirt her young calves to keep them clean too.

Fierce And Ferocious

Watch out for the **tiger**, with its big teeth, strong jaws and long, sharp claws. The tiger hunts wild pigs and antelope. But people who live near tigers know they should stay away too!

Here's a hug nobody wants! The **python** squeezes its prey with its powerful body. It tightens its squeeze until the animal stops breathing.

The **squid** needs huge eyes to see in its deep water home. With two long tentacles and eight enormous arms, it catches other sea creatures for dinner.

42

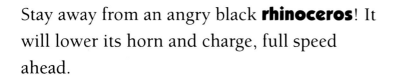

Stay away from an angry black **rhinoceros**! It will lower its horn and charge, full speed ahead.

The **cobra** bites with deadly poison to capture its prey or to protect itself.

A male **lion** looks and sounds fierce. But the hunters in the family are the females, the lionesses. After the hunt, the females stand back and let the male lion eat first.

Its razor-sharp teeth make this **great white shark** a killer. It snatches up seals, sea lions, dolphins, turtles and other sharks. Great whites have even attacked boats and people.

Moms, Dads, And Babies

The **Emperor penguin** mom lays the egg, but it is dad that keeps it warm. Dad waits for the egg to hatch, holding it between his feet and under a fold of skin.

A **gorilla** mom cares for her baby much as a human mom does. The baby's older brothers and sisters may also help clean it, feed it, play with it and cuddle it.

When a **shrew** mom takes her babies for a walk, they form a long line. Each baby holds tightly to the tail ahead of it.

A **cichlid fish** mom carries her eggs in her mouth. When they have hatched, mom blows the babies out. But they return to mom's mouth at night, or when danger threatens.

After the **midwife toad** mom lays eggs, the dad keeps them safe from danger by wrapping them around his legs. He carries the eggs wherever he goes until they hatch. This makes walking difficult.

A **kangaroo** mom carries her baby in a pouch on the outside of her tummy. What a bouncy bed for baby!

Polar bear babies need a safe, warm place when they are first born. So mom digs a deep cave in the snow. After about four months, the babies will be strong enough to survive the bitter cold outside.

Even fierce **crocodiles** have moms. When the babies hatch, a crocodile mom gently carries them in her mouth from their sandy nest to the river where they will live.